One little bunny bounces a ball.

Two little bunnies play on the seesaw.

Three little bunnies fly a kite.

Four little bunnies swing on a swing.

Five little bunnies play soccer.

Six little bunnies jump rope.

Seven little bunnies play with a shuttlecock.

Eight little bunnies build a sandcastle.

Nine little bunnies slide down the slide.

Ten little bunnies play games together.